Diet recommendations during TCM - Liver - Wind with Extreme Heat

Please check these recommendations always with a nutrition consultant, therapist, doctor or dietician. The recipes and the list of ingredients are supporting the conventional medical therapy. The calorie disclosures of fresh ingredients (fruit and vegetables) vary according to quality and time of harvest. The contents were checked by a dietician and a nutrition consultant for the Traditional Chinese Medicine (TCM).

Author:
©2020 Josef Miligui
www.ebns.at

AF220848

Source:
The lists are created from the EBNS database for nutritional counseling. The database is used by dietitians, therapists and doctors for advising the patient / client.

Literature:
The specialist literature and the training documents of the German and Austrian dietary and traditional Chinese medicine serve as a knowledge base. We have used the documents as a basis of knowledge, adapted it to our experience and completed them.
http://nutribook.info/

Production and publishing:
BoD – Books on Demand, Norderstedt
ISBN: 9783752830965

Diet recommendations for TCM - Liver - Wind with Extreme Heat

1   Treatment strategy

n.a.

2   Avoid

n.a.

3   Breakfast

	kkal. per serving
Boiled celery salad with exotic spices	165
Celery juice	33
Celery soup	101
Champignon rice	410
Cucumber soup	95
Kohlrabi in chervil sauce with potatoes	187
Noodles with vegetable and tomato sauce	561
Raw celery salad	590
Spinach with cottage cheese	263
Tea from celery sticks	1
Tea from sage	4
Wheat fresh grain porridge with pears.	309

4   Snack

Kohlrabi Potatoes mash - also for babies from 8 months..................278

5 Lunch

6 Afternoon

7 Dinner

8 Any time

9 Recipes

(rec.) = You can use more.
(little) = You should use less than specified
(omit) = omit.

9.1 Apple and celery soup with roasted fennel

Strengthens spleen and liver, strengthens stomach Qi, spreads, directs down, warms the inside, lowers cold.
Cooking time approx. 1 hour
Calories p. portion: 191
5 portions
Allergens: L

Quantity of ingredients
Celery root 1 piece / 350g. (rec.) - cool - sweet ....earth
Apple (sour) 1 piece / 175g. (little) - cool - sour ....wood
Onion white 1 piece / 100g. (little) - warm - acrid......................................metal
Rapeseed oil 2 table spoons / 20g. (rec.) - neutral - sweet........................earth
Basic recipe for a vegetable soup 2 1/4 cups / 600g. (rec.) - neutral - * ....*
Fennel 1 piece / 150g. () - warm - sweet, little acrid..................................earth
Salt 1 pinch / 0,5g. (yes) - cold - salty ....water
Pepper (ground) 1 pinch / 0,1g. () - warm - acrid ....metal
 1/2 cup / 100g. (yes) - neutral - sweet, bitter...water

Cooking instructions:
Peel onion and celery and dice roughly. Peel the apple, quarter, remove the core, cut the apple into cubes.
Heat half of the oil in a large saucepan and fry the onion cubes in a medium heat for 2-3 minutes.
Add pieces of celery and pieces of apple and simmer for 1 minute. Add the vegetable broth according to the basic recipe, boil everything and cook over a low heat for about 45 minutes.
In the meantime, clean the fennel, wash and drain. Finely chop the fennel.
Heat a pan, add remaining oil and roast the fennel cubes in medium

heat, stirring constantly, until well browned and tender. Season with salt and pepper and keep warm. Puree the soup ingredients in the broth with a hand blender. Brush apple celery soup through a sieve and pour it back into the pot. Add soy cream and heat everything again for about 1 minute. Season the apple and celery soup with salt and pepper. Spread in the soup plate and serve garnished with the roasted fennel.

9.2   Asparagus and herb ragout

Nourishes Yin from lung kidney blood and liver, produces humors, feeds Yin, moisturizes, relaxes, builds up Qi, spreads, strengthens spleen and liver, regulates Qi flow.
Cooking time approx. 30 min
Calories p. portion: 168
4 portions
Allergens: GL

Quantity of ingredients
Basic recipe for a vegetable soup 2 cups / 500g. (rec.) - neutral - * ....*
Lemon peel 1/2 piece / 3g. (yes) - cool - bitter .... fire
Coriander 1/4 teaspoon / 1g. (little) - warm - acrid .... metal
Nutmeg 1 pinch / 0,3g. () - warm - acrid... metal
Asparagus (green or white) 1,8 lbs / 800g. (rec.) - cool - sweet, bitter....... earth
Parsley 1 Bunch / 125g. () - warm - bitter..wood
Créme fraiche cheese 2 table spoons / 30g. (yes) - neutral - sweet ....earth
Lemon juice 1 teaspoon / 3g. (yes) - cold - sour ....wood
Potato 7/8 lbs / 400g. (rec.) - neutral - sweet .... earth

Cooking instructions:
Cook potatoes with plenty of salted water about 20 min. until soft.
Heat the vegetable stock with lemon zest, coriander and nutmeg till it boil. Cook the peeled and sliced asparagus in it.
Drain asparagus in a sieve. Collect the cooking liquid.
In the blender mix 200 g of cooked asparagus (the lower ends), cooking liquid and parsley to a smooth sauce. Beat the sauce with crème fraîche until smooth. Add asparagus and heat again and season with lemon juice, salt and pepper. Serve with the potatoes.

9.3   Asparagus Cream Soup

Nourishes Yin from lung and kidney, produces humors, feeds Yin, moisturizes, relaxes, builds up Qi, spreads. moisturizes, laxative, antiparasitic, nourishes blood and liver, harmonizes liver and spleen, nourishes Yin from heart and kidney.
Cooking time approx. 45 min
Calories p. portion: 240
2 portions
Allergens: ACG

Quantity of ingredients
Asparagus (green or white) 5/8 oz / 200g. (rec.) - cool - sweet, bitter .... earth
Water 2 cup / 500g. (yes) - cool - salty... earth
Rapeseed oil 3 table spoons / 30g. (rec.) - neutral - sweet......................... earth
Wheat flour 2 table spoons / 10g. (rec.) - cool - sweet, salty .... wood
Chicken yolk 1 piece / 25g. (yes) - neutral - sweet.................................... earth
Cow's milk (3.5% fat) 1 table spoon / 15g. (little) - neutral - sweet............. earth
Sour cream 15% fat 1 table spoon / 15g. (little) - cool - sour .... wood
Pepper (ground) 1 pinch / 0,5g. () - warm - acrid .... metal
Nutmeg 1 pinch / 0,5g. () - warm - acrid... metal
Lemon juice 1 teaspoon / 2g. (yes) - cold - sour .... wood
Parsley 2 table spoons / 20g. () - warm - bitter .... wood
Salt 1 pinch / 1g. (yes) - cold - salty .... water

Cooking instructions:
Wash and peel the asparagus.
Heat water, a little lemon juice and pinch of salt till it boils. Tie the asparagus spears together.
Add the asparagus peel to the cooking water and bring to the boil.
Add the asparagus and cook on low heat for about 20 minutes.
Then remove the asparagus bunches and pour the broth through a sieve.
For the roux, heat the oil in a saucepan, add the flour and sauté until it is colorless, slowly top up with the asparagus sauce and simmer for 10 minutes. Cut the asparagus spears into pieces about 3 cm long and place them to the soup.

Just before serving, bring the soup to the boil again.
Mix the egg yolk with the milk and sour cream.
Remove the pot from the heat and stir in the egg yolk and milk mixture.
Season with pepper and nutmeg, decorate with the chopped parsley and serve immediately.

9.4 Basic recipe for a vegetable soup, nutritious

Strengthens spleen and lung, regulates Qi flow, builds up Qi, dries out, passes downwardly, strengthens stomach Qi.
Cooking time approx. 2-3 hours
Calories p. portion: 48
5 portions
Allergens: L

Quantity of ingredients
Olive oil 1 table spoon / 4g. (rec.) - cool - sweet .... earth
Onion white 1 piece / 60g. (little) - warm - acrid .... metal
Carrot 3 pieces / 200g. () - neutral - sweet.. earth
Parsnip 3/8 lbs - 6oz / 150g. (rec.) - cool - bitter .... fire
Celery root 1 cup / 100g. (rec.) - cool - sweet .... earth
Ginger fresh 1/2 teaspoon / 2g. (little) - warm - acrid .... metal
Lemon 1/2 piece / 25g. (yes) - cold - sour...wood
Juniper berry 6 pieces / 6g. () - warm - sweet, acrid, bitter .... fire
Thyme dried 1 pinch / 1g. () - warm - bitter .... metal
Lovage 1 table spoon / 3g. () - warm - acrid, bitter................................... metal
Bay leaf 2 leaves / 1g. (little) - warm - acrid ....*
Salt 1 pinch / 1g. (yes) - cold - salty .... water
Water 3 cups / 650g. (yes) - cool - salty.. earth

Cooking instructions:
Cut the vegetables into cubes.
Heat oil in hot pot, fry shortly onions and vegetables.
Add cold water, then add ginger, bay leaf and lemon juice.
Season with juniper, thyme and lovage. Cover for 2 - 3 hours on a low heat and simmer.
The used vegetables should be thrown away.
The basic recipe serves as a soup base and to refine vegetables, legumes or cereals.
If you want to eat vegetable soup immediately, add the desired vegetables half an hour before.
Refrigerate for later use.

9.5 Boiled celery salad with exotic spices

Strengthens stomach Qi, builds up Qi, moisturises dryness, preserves the fluids, cools heat.
Cooking time approx. 30 min
Calories p. portion: 166
4 portions
Allergens: GLMNO

Quantity of ingredients

Celery root 1 1/2 piece / 900g. (rec.) - cool - sweet .... earth
Yogurt (natural, 3.5% fat) 1 cup / 250g. (yes) - cool - sour ....wood
Sour cream 15% fat 2 table spoons / 20g. (little) - cool - sour ....wood
Turmeric (yellow root) 1 pinch / 1g. (yes) - warm - bitter..................................*
Sesame oil 1 table spoon / 20g. (rec.) - cool - sweet .... earth
Pepper (ground) 1 pinch / 0,5g. () - warm - acrid .... metal
Onion white 1/2 piece / 25g. (little) - warm - acrid .... metal
Black caraway 1 pinch / 1g. (rec.) - warm - acrid, sweet..................................*
Salt 1 pinch / 1g. (yes) - cold - salty .... water
Lemon juice 1 piece / 40g. (yes) - cold - sour ....wood
Apple (sour) 1/2 piece / 100g. (little) - cool - sour ....wood
Vinegar (Apple vinegar) 1 dash / 3g. () - warm - sour, bitter ....wood

Cooking instructions:

Cook the peeled celeriac in thick slices and then cut into bite-sized strips.
Dressing: Mix a little yoghurt, sour cream, turmeric, sesame oil, pepper, lemongrass powder, finely chopped onion, a little mustard, salt, crushed black cumin, some cold water, lemon juice or vinegar; add the sour chopped apple, some rose paprika, the lukewarm celery and mix well; let it rest for 2 - 3 hours or overnight.
Ideal as a substitute for raw food

9.6   Celery and potato cream soup

Strengthens spleen and liver, regulates Qi flow, strengthens stomach Qi, forces Qi, relieves inflammation, relaxes, dissolves stagnation.
Cooking time approx. 45 min
Calories p. portion: 113
4 portions
Allergens: GL

Quantity of ingredients

Olive oil 1 table spoon / 10g. (rec.) - cool - sweet .... earth
Onion white 1/2 piece / 25g. (little) - warm - acrid .... metal
Basic recipe for a vegetable soup 3 cups / 700g. (rec.) - neutral - * ....*
Potato 5/8 oz / 200g. (rec.) - neutral - sweet .... earth
Nutmeg 1 pinch / 0,5g. () - warm - acrid... metal
Ground 1 pinch / 0,5g. (little) - warm - acrid .... metal
Lemon peel 1/4 piece / 1g. (yes) - cool - bitter .... fire
Créme fraiche cheese 2 table spoons / 20g. (yes) - neutral - sweet .... earth
Salt 1 pinch / 1g. (yes) - cold - salty .... water
Parsley 1 table spoon / 8g. () - warm - bitter ....wood

Cooking instructions:
Heat the olive oil in a saucepan lightly. Fry the onions very gently in a mild heat. Pour with vegetable stock according to the basic recipe. Cover and cook for 15 minutes.
Add curd-cut potato, celery, nutmeg, cumin and lemon zest. Spice with salt and cook for 12 minutes. Potatoes and celery should be soft. Remove the lemon peel.
Puree the soup with crème fraiche using a blender. Season the soup with salt.
Arrange the soup in portions with the chopped parsley.

9.7 Celery juice

Strengthens stomach Qi, moisturizes, relaxes, builds up Qi, spreads.
Cooking time approx. 5 min
Calories p. portion: 33
1 portions
Allergens: L

Quantity of ingredients
Celery root 1/2 piece / 200g. (rec.) - cool - sweet .... earth
Water 1 cup / 120g. (yes) - cool - salty.. earth
Salt 1 pinch / 0,5g. (yes) - cold - salty .... water

Cooking instructions:
Peel celeriac and cut into pieces and juice. Mix with water and salt as needed.
Celery salad with lemon and olive oil
Strengthens stomach Qi, moisturizes, relaxes, builds up Qi.
Cooking time approx. 10 min
Calories p. portion: 402
1 portions
Allergens: L

Quantity of ingredients
Celery root 1/2 piece / 200g. (rec.) - cool - sweet .... earth
Lemon juice 1/2 piece / 10g. (yes) - cold - sour ....wood
Olive oil 4 table spoons / 40g. (rec.) - cool - sweet .... earth

Cooking instructions:
Peel celeriac and cut into pieces and rub. Serve with the lemon juice and olive oil.

9.8   Celery soup

Refreshing, builds up fluids and Qi.
Cooking time approx. 45 min
Calories p. portion: 101
4 portions
Allergens: ACGL

Quantity of ingredients

Water 2 cup / 500g. (yes) - cool - salty..earth
Butter organic 1 table spoon / 15g. (rec.) - neutral - sweet ....earth
Nutmeg 1 pinch / 1g. () - warm - acrid ....metal
Salt 1 pinch / 1g. (yes) - cold - salty ....water
Spelled wholemeal flour 2-3 teaspoons / 25g. (little) - neutral - sweet.......wood
Celery root 1 piece / 500g. (rec.) - cool - sweet ....earth
Chicken egg 1 piece / 55g. (rec.) - neutral - sweet.....................................earth
Cream sour 10% 2 table spoons / 25g. (little) - neutral - sweet ....earth
Celery sticks 2 table spoons / 20g. (rec.) - cool - sweet.............................earth
Pepper (ground) 1 pinch / 0,5g. () - warm - acrid ....metal

Cooking instructions:

In a hot saucepan, melt 1 tbsp butter; add a pinch of nutmeg, a pinch of salt, 1/2 cup wholegrain spelled flour (finely ground as fresh as possible) and stir to a sweat while stirring; add 1/2 liter of hot water gradually; add 1 large finely chopped celery tuber; cook for about 35 minutes and then puree; mix 1 egg yolk with 1 cup of cream; in the hot - no longer boiling! - soup vigorously; add some celery leaves finely chopped; with pepper, salt to taste.

9.9   Champignon rice

Strengthens spleen, builds up Qi, directs heat down, strengthens stomach Qi, cools blood heat.
Cooking time approx. 30 min
Calories p. portion: 410
2 portions
Allergens: L

Quantity of ingredients

Onion white 1 piece / 50g. (little) - warm - acrid ....metal
Bay leaf 2 pieces / 1g. (little) - warm - acrid ....*
Clove 2 pieces / 1g. (little) - warm - acrid ....metal
Basic recipe for a vegetable soup 7/8 lbs / 350g. (rec.) - neutral - * ....*

Rice (whole grain) 5/8 oz / 200g. (yes) - warm - sweet .... metal
Champignon 1/8 lbs - 2oz / 60g. (rec.) - cool - sweet................................. earth
Parsley 1/2 oz / 20g. () - warm - bitter ....wood
Pepper (ground) 1 pinch / 0,2g. () - warm - acrid .... metal

Cooking instructions:
Plug in the cloves in the onion. Heat the vegetable stock with the onion
and the bay leaves till it boils. Add the rice to the boiling liquid, reduce
the temperature to the lowest level and stir with the lid closed for 20-25
minutes.
In the meantime, wash the mushrooms, clean them, slice them, sauté
briefly with a little water or sauté. Wash the parsley and chop finely.
Remove the onion from the rice, add the mushrooms and the parsley,
season with pepper.

9.10 Champignon salad with cress

Cools blood heat.
Cooking time approx. 5 min
Calories p. portion: 220
1 portions
Allergens: AN

Quantity of ingredients
Champignon 5/8 lbs - 8oz / 250g. (rec.) - cool - sweet................................ earth
Sesame oil 2 table spoons / 6g. (rec.) - cool - sweet .... earth
Pepper (ground) 1 pinch / 0,5g. () - warm - acrid .... metal
Salt 1 pinch / 1g. (yes) - cold - salty .... water
Lemon 1/2 piece / 15g. (yes) - cold - sour...wood
Cress 2 table spoons / 10g. (yes) - cool - sweet .... metal
White bread (wheat bread) 2 slices / 30g. (yes) - cool - sweet ....wood

Cooking instructions:
Cut mushrooms into thin slices.
Dressing: sesame oil, a little ground pepper, salt, plenty of lemon juice,
stir well the rose pepper; give over the finely chopped mushrooms;
plenty of watercress.
Goes well with: white bread, round grain rice or quinoa; Along with the
cereal, the salad makes a simple, light meal.
Serve with white bread.

9.11 Cucumber soup

Cools and moisturizes, diuretic, reduces damp heat, detoxifies, relaxes, builds up Qi, spreads, distributes mucus, passes downwardly, activates Wei Qi, forces Qi.
Cooking time approx. 20 min
Calories p. portion: 96
4 portions
Allergens: M

Quantity of ingredients
Olive oil 2 table spoons / 35g. (rec.) - cool - sweet .... earth
Cucumber 2 pieces / 400g. (rec.) - cold - sweet .... earth
Water 2 cup / 500g. (yes) - cool - salty .... earth
Sage 3 leaves / 3g. (rec.) - neutral - bitter, spicy .... fire
Coriander 1 pinch / 1g. (little) - warm - acrid .... metal
Cardamom 1 pinch / 1g. () - warm - acrid .... *
Salt 1 pinch / 1g. (yes) - cold - salty .... water

Cooking instructions:
Heat oil and roast short the small cucumbers. Add Mustard seeds, coriander, cardamom and salt. Add water. Simmer for 10-15 min. Puree and decorate with fresh chopped sage.

9.12 Kohlrabi in chervil sauce with potatoes

Forces Qi, forces spleen, relieves inflammation, relaxes, spreads, moves Qi and blood, diuretic, strengthens spleen and liver, regulates Qi flow, cools heat, reduces internal wind and moisture, dissolves stagnation, directs upwards.
Cooking time approx. 1 hour
Calories p. portion: 188
4 portions
Allergens: GL

Quantity of ingredients
Potato 6 pieces / 450g. (rec.) - neutral - sweet .... earth
Basic recipe for a vegetable soup 1 cup / 300g. (rec.) - neutral - * .... *
Potato 1/4 lbs - 4oz / 100g. (rec.) - neutral - sweet .... earth

Nutmeg 1 pinch / 0,2g. () - warm - acrid .... metal
Lemon peel 1/2 teaspoon / 2g. (yes) - cool - bitter .... fire
Ginger fresh 1/2 teaspoon / 2g. (little) - warm - acrid .... metal
Lovage 1/2 teaspoon / 2g. () - warm - acrid, bitter .... metal
Kohlrabi 3/4 lbs / 300g. (rec.) - neutral - acrid, sweet................................ earth
Salt 1 pinch / 1g. (yes) - cold - salty .... water
Pepper (ground) 1 pinch / 0,2g. () - warm - acrid .... metal
Sour cream 15% fat 3 table spoons / 30g. (little) - cool - sour ....wood
Chervil dried 1 Bunch / 80g. (rec.) - warm - sweet ....*

Cooking instructions:
Boil the potatoes in salted water.
Bring half of the vegetable stock to boil. Add the diced potatoes,
nutmeg, lemon zest, ginger and lovage. Cover the potatoes and cook
for about 10 minutes until soft and puree them with a blender until they
are smooth.
Bring remaining vegetable stock to boil. Cut kohlrabi into cubes and
add, cover and cook for about 8 minutes. Stir in the potato sauce and
heat everything briefly.
Puree with the mixing stick chervil and sour cream. Mix the chervil
cream with the kohlrabi vegetables.
Serve with the cooked, peeled potatoes.

9.13 Kohlrabi Potatoes mash - also for babies from 8 months

Moves Qi and blood, reduces moisture, forces Qi, forces spleen,
relieves inflammation, moisturizes, relaxes, builds up Qi, spreads,
forces kidney Jing.
Cooking time approx. 25 min
Calories p. portion: 278
1 portions
Allergens: CG

Quantity of ingredients
Kohlrabi 1/2 piece / 150g. (rec.) - neutral - acrid, sweet............................ earth
Potato 1/4 lbs - 4oz / 100g. (rec.) - neutral - sweet .... earth
Butter organic 1 table spoon / 10g. (rec.) - neutral - sweet .... earth
Chicken yolk 1 piece / 25g. (yes) - neutral - sweet.................................... earth

Cooking instructions:
Remove the kohlrabi leaves, wash the tuber and tender leaves and the potatoes thoroughly. Peel the kohlrabi and potatoes, cut into cubes about 1 cm in size. Melt half the butter in a small saucepan, add the kohlrabi and the potatoes and fry in it. Steam with 2 tablespoons of water in a closed saucepan over low heat for about 15 minutes. Meanwhile, free the tenderest kohlrabi leaves from the stems and chop very finely. In total, at most 2 tablespoons of leaf pieces should be used. Add this to the vegetables about 5 minutes before the end of the cooking time. Stir in the egg yolk and bring to the boil again. Put the vegetables in a plate and mix with the remaining butter and egg yolk. (Crush for the baby with a fork.)

9.14 Nettle-chard soup

Drains moisture down, strengthens blood, cools liver heat.
Cooking time approx. 30 min
Calories p. portion: 52
4 portions

Quantity of ingredients
Nettles Handful / 10g. (little) - neutral - bitter...wood
Chard 1 lbs / 500g. (yes) - cool - bitter, sweet...earth
Salt 1 pinch / 1g. (yes) - cold - salty .... water
Water 2 cup / 400g. (yes) - cool - salty..earth
Olive oil 1 table spoon / 10g. (rec.) - cool - sweet ....earth
Pepper (ground) 1 pinch / 0,5g. () - warm - acrid .... metal

Cooking instructions:
Heat the oil in a saucepan, add the washed and finely chopped Swiss chard. Salt and let simmer for 10 minutes. Add the chopped nettles and cook for another 10 minutes. Add pepper and puree.

9.15 Noodles with vegetable and tomato sauce

Nourishes liver-Yin, produces humors, cools blood, reduces mucus, moisturizes, relaxes, builds up Qi, spreads.
Cooking time approx. 45 min
Calories p. portion: 562
2 portions
Allergens: ACG

Quantity of ingredients

Tomato 1/4 lbs - 4oz / 125g. (rec.) - cold - sweet-sour..................................wood
Carrot 1 piece / 80g. () - neutral - sweet...earth
Zucchini 1 piece / 80g. (rec.) - cool - sweet...earth
Olive oil 1 table spoon / 15g. (rec.) - cool - sweet ....earth
Onion (shallot) 1 piece / 20g. () - warm - acrid, sweet............................. metal
Oregano dried 1 pinch / 1g. () - warm - bitter .... metal
Salt 1 pinch / 1g. (yes) - cold - salty .... water
Pepper (ground) 1 pinch / 0,2g. () - warm - acrid .... metal
Noodles (wheat) with egg 5/8 oz / 200g. (rec.) - cool - sweet, salty...........wood
Olive oil 1 table spoon / 10g. (rec.) - cool - sweet ....earth
Créme fraiche cheese 2 table spoons / 30g. (yes) - neutral - sweet .... earth

Cooking instructions:

Boil the tomatoes with a little water, drain and collect the juice, cut the
tomatoes into pieces.
Roughly grate zucchini and carrot. Heat olive oil in a pot. Steam shallots
very soft. Add tomatoes, season with oregano, salt and pepper. Simmer
tomatoes to a thick sauce.
Bring plenty of salted water to boil, cook the wholegrain noodles until
firm. In the cooking time of the pasta, heat in a pan olive oil. Fry the
carrots while stirring, lightly salt. Add zucchini, sauté briefly while
stirring. The vegetables should be soft with a bite.
Drain pasta, mix with créme fraiche, season with salt and pepper.
Garnish with the tomato sauce.

9.16 Paprika-tomato rice

Strengthens spleen and liver, regulates Qi flow, warms the stomach and
spleen, harmonizes the intestine, forces Qi, nourishes liver-Yin, cools
heat, produces humors, warms stomach, relaxes, builds up Qi, spreads.
Cooking time approx. 25 min
Calories p. portion: 291
3 portions
Allergens: L

Quantity of ingredients

Onion white 1 piece / 50g. (little) - warm - acrid .... metal
Peppers 4 pieces / 120g. (rec.) - cool - sweet..earth
Bay leaf 2 pieces / 1g. (little) - warm - acrid ....*
Clove 2 pieces / 1g. (little) - warm - acrid .... metal

Basic recipe for a vegetable soup 7/8 lbs / 400g. (rec.) - neutral - * ....*
Rice (whole grain) 5/8 oz / 200g. (yes) - warm - sweet .... metal
Champignon 1/8 lbs - 2oz / 60g. (rec.) - cool - sweet................................. earth
Parsley 1/2 oz / 20g. () - warm - bitter ....wood
Pepper (ground) 1 pinch / 0,2g. () - warm - acrid .... metal
Peppers (rose peppers) 1 pinch / 0,2g. (rec.) - warm - bitter .... earth
Tomato 1/4 lbs - 4oz / 120g. (rec.) - cold - sweet-sour................................wood

Cooking instructions:
Finely chop the onion. Cut the peppers into fine strips.
Heat margarine in a saucepan, sauté onions and peppers, and rice.
Add the vegetable stock, add cloves and bay leaves and leave to
simmer in a closed pot for approx. 20 minutes. Cut the tomato meat into
1 cm cubes and add to the rice 5 minutes before the end of cooking.

9.17 Raw celery salad

Strengthens stomach Qi, moisturizes, relaxes, builds up Qi, spreads,
cools heat, nourishes fluids, keeps fluids, reduces internal wind, forces
stomach, forces Qi, forces liver and kidney.
Cooking time approx. 15 min
Calories p. portion: 590
1 portions
Allergens: HLN

Quantity of ingredients
Celery root 1/4 piece / 125g. (rec.) - cool - sweet .... earth
Celery sticks 2 branches / 30g. (rec.) - cool - sweet .... earth
Sesame oil 4 table spoons / 40g. (rec.) - cool - sweet .... earth
Almond puree 2 table spoons / 20g. () - neutral - sweet .... earth
Pepper (ground) 1 pinch / 0,5g. () - warm - acrid .... metal
Salt 1 pinch / 1g. (yes) - cold - salty .... water
Lemon 1/2 cup / 50g. (yes) - cold - sour..wood
Orange juice 1/2 cup / 60g. (yes) - cold - sour, sweet................................wood

Cooking instructions:
Finely grate the celeriac; cut the celeriac into small pieces; celery
leaves, cut into small pieces, blanch and combine
 everything.

Dressing: sesame oil, almond paste, pepper, salt, lemon and fresh
orange juice, stir well some rose paprika; mix with the celery and let it
pass through.

9.18 Spinach soup with mascarpone

Nourishes blood and yin, strengthens zang-organs, strengthens the gastrointestinal tract, harmonizes qi, relieves
 alcohol poisoning, moisturizes lungs. Strengthens spleen and liver, regulates Qi flow, relaxes, builds up Qi.
Cooking time approx. 30 min
Calories p. portion: 928
4 portions
Allergens: AGL

Quantity of ingredients
Butter (half fat) 1/8 lbs - 2oz / 60g. (yes) - neutral - sweet .... earth
Onion (spring onion) 1 Bunch / 200g. (little) - warm - acrid .... metal
Spinach 3/4 lbs / 350g. (rec.) - cool - sweet, rough .... earth
Basic recipe for a vegetable soup 3 1/2 cups / 800g. (rec.) - neutral - * ....*
Celery sticks 2 pieces / 60g. (rec.) - cool - sweet .... earth
Mascarpone cheese 5/8 lbs - 8 oz / 225g. () - neutral - sweet .... earth
Salt 1 pinch / 1g. (yes) - cold - salty .... water
Pepper (ground) 1 pinch / 0,5g. () - warm - acrid .... metal
Olive oil 1 table spoon / 10g. (rec.) - cool - sweet .... earth
Ground 1/2 teaspoon / 2g. (little) - warm - acrid .... metal
Spelled (Dark) bread 2 slices / 20g. (little) - neutral - sweet........................wood

Cooking instructions:
Melt half of the butter in a saucepan over medium heat. Add chopped green onion and small celery stalks for about
 5 minutes.
Add the spinach to the saucepan, add the stock and heat till it boils, then cook on a low heat for 15-20 minutes.
Purée the soup. Stir in the mascarpone evenly, season with salt and pepper.
Croutons: Heat the remaining butter with the olive oil in a pan. Roast diced bread over medium heat while turning frequently until golden brown. Just before the end of the roasting season, mix in the caraway.
Arrange the soup in bowls and sprinkle the croutons over it.

9.19 Spinach with cottage cheese

Refreshing, builds up fluids, forces Qi, forces spleen, relieves inflammation, moisturizes, relaxes.
Cooking time approx. 10 min
Calories p. portion: 263
1 portions
Allergens: GN

Quantity of ingredients

Sesame oil 1 table spoon / 10g. (rec.) - cool - sweet .... earth
Onion white 1/2 piece / 40g. (little) - warm - acrid .... metal
Garlic 1/2clove / 1g. () - hot - acrid .... metal
Spinach 2 handful / 150g. (rec.) - cool - sweet, rough............................... earth
Pepper (ground) 1 pinch / 0,2g. () - warm - acrid .... metal
Nutmeg 1 pinch / 0,2g. () - warm - acrid... metal
Salt 1 pinch / 0,5g. (yes) - cold - salty .... water
Potato 4 pieces / 200g. (rec.) - neutral - sweet .... earth
Sour cream 15% fat 2 table spoons / g. (little) - cool - sour .... wood
Salt 1 pinch / 0,3g. (yes) - cold - salty .... water

Cooking instructions:

Heat in a pot sesame oil, add finely chopped onion, roast glassy; fry a
little garlic; stew in strips of spinach for about 3 minutes; add ground
pepper, nutmeg, salt, a bit of sour cream as desired or serve the
spinach with a large dollop of cottage cheese as an appetizer.
In addition, boil the potatoes in salted water, then peel.

9.20 Spinach with Tahini

Nourishes blood and Yin, forces Zang-organs, forces stomach and
intestines, harmonizes Qi, moisturizes lungs, forces Qi, forces spleen,
relieves inflammation, moisturizes, relaxes, builds up Qi, spreads,
nourishes blood.
Cooking time approx. 20 min
Calories p. portion: 150
4 portions
Allergens: N

Quantity of ingredients

Potato 1,1 lbs / 500g. (rec.) - neutral - sweet .... earth
Salt 1 pinch / 0,2g. (yes) - cold - salty .... water
Water 1 cup / 25g. (yes) - cool - salty... earth
Spinach 2,2 lbs / 800g. (rec.) - cool - sweet, rough.................................... earth

Cooking instructions:

Cook potatoes and peel. Heat water. Blanch spinach. Shake off water
and let it dry and stir with sesame.

9.21 Tea from celery sticks

Brings the Liver Qi in motion, cools heat, moisturizes, relaxes, builds up Qi, spreads.
Cooking time approx. 15 min
Calories p. portion: 1
4 portions
Allergens: L

Quantity of ingredients
Celery sticks 2 table spoons (chopped) / 18g. (rec.) - cool - sweet............ earth
Water 2 cup / 500g. (yes) - cool - salty.. earth

Cooking instructions:
Heat the water till it boils and put it aside. Add cutted celery and cook for 10 min. to let go. Strain. Sweet to taste with honey.

9.22 Tea from chamomile

Reduces internal wind and heat, cools liver.
Cooking time approx. 10 min
Calories p. portion: 0
1 portions

Quantity of ingredients
Chamomile 1 teaspoon / 3g. (rec.) - cool - sweet, bitter.....................................*
Water 1 cup / 120g. (yes) - cool - salty.. earth

Cooking instructions:
Heat the water till it boils and put it aside. Chamomile flowers added and 10 min. to let go.

9.23 Tea from sage

Distributes mucus, passes downwardly, activates Wei Qi, forces Qi.
Cooking time approx. 15 min
Calories p. portion: 4
4 portions

Quantity of ingredients
Sage 2 teaspoons / 6g. (rec.) - neutral - bitter, spicy .... fire
Water 2 cup / 500g. (yes) - cool - salty.. earth

Cooking instructions:
Heat the water till it boils and put it aside. Add sage and 10 min. to let go. Strain. Sweet to taste with honey.

9.24 Wheat fresh grain porridge with pears.

Moisturizes lungs, cools heat, reduces lung mucus, nourishes Yin from heart and kidney, forces heart and kidney, moisturizes, relaxes, builds up Qi, spreads.
Cooking time approx. 25 min
Calories p. portion: 309
2 portions
Allergens: ANO

Quantity of ingredients
Wheat 1 cup / 100g. (rec.) - cool - sweet ....wood
Water 2-4 cups / 350g. (yes) - cool - salty... earth
Pear 2 pieces / 300g. (rec.) - cool - sweet, sour... earth
Raisins 1 table spoon / 10g. () - warm - sweet .... earth
Sesame, white 1 table spoon / 8g. (yes) - neutral - sweet .... earth
Sunflower seeds 1 table spoon / 8g. (yes) - neutral - sweet .... earth
Cardamom 1 pinch / 0,3g. () - warm - acrid.. *
Salt 1 pinch / 0,3g. (yes) - cold - salty .... water

Cooking instructions:
Preparation the night before: Wheat roughly cut; soak overnight.

In the morning: Put the wheat meal with a little hot water; simmer with stirring for about 15 minutes.
Meanwhile, add pear compote, raisins, crushed sesame, sunflower seeds, some ground cardamom, a small pinch of salt.

Variants: with grated apple or seasonal fruit.

10 Effects of food

10.1 Use ingredients: recommendable

Agar agar (kelp)
Apple (sweet)
Arrowroot
Artichoke
Asparagus (green or white)
Aubergine
Balm
Basic recipe for a vegetable soup (nutritious)
Bearberry leaf
Beef liver
Beef meat (calf)
Beer (Pils)
Beer (Top-fermented German dark beer)
Bitter melon
Black caraway
Boletus mushroom
Broad beans (thick beans)
Broccoli
Brussels sprouts
Buckwheat
Buckwheat (roasted) Kasha
Buckwheat whole grain
Butter organic
Calamari
Carp
Cashews
Cauliflower
Celery root
Celery sticks
Chamomile
Champignon
Chanterelle
Chervil
Chervil dried
Chicken egg
Chicken egg white
Chicken stomach
Chickpeas
Chicory
Chinese cabbage
Chlorella (fresh water)
Chrysanthemum blossom tea
Coconut flakes
Coconut grated

Coconut meat
Coix (seeds) YiYi Ren
Corn
Corn (fast polenta)
Corn flour
Corn Grease (Polenta)
Corn silk tea
Crucian
Cucumber
Dandelion (young plants)
Duck (heart)
Duck (slaughtered)
Elderberry blossom tee
Endive salad
Fig
Fig dried
Fish pieces mixed (fresh water)
Gentian root
Goose
Goose parts
Gourd
Grape juice red
Grape juice white
Grapes red
Green tea
Hazelnuts
Herring
Hibiscus
Hop
Iceberg lettuce
Jasmine blossoms tee
Kaki plum
Kohlrabi
Kombu seaweed (Saccharina japonica)
Leaf salads (bitter)
Lentils black
Lentils red
Lotus roots
Malt
Margarine
Margarine (diet)
Millet
Millet flakes
Morel (black, dried)
Morel, dried
Mung bean

Nasturtium (nose-twister or nose-tweaker)
Noodles (wheat) with egg
Octopus
Olive oil
Oyster shell powder
Oysters
Parsnip
Passion blossoms tea
Peanut oil
Peanuts
Pear
Peas, green
Peppers
Peppers (rose peppers)
Peppers (sweet)
Perch
Pine nuts
Pistachios
Potato
Potato (mealy)
Potato flour
Pumpkin seeds
Quail
Quail egg
Quince
Quinoa
Radicchio
Rapeseed oil
Red cabbage
Reishi mushroom
Rice Basmati
Rice long grain rice
Romaine lettuce / lettuce salad
Rye
Rye flour
Rye wholemeal bread
Saffron
Sage

Salmon
Savory
Sesame oil
Shark
Shiitake, dried
Soy Tofu
Soybean milk
Soybeans, black
Soybeans, yellow
Spinach
Sugar substitute (sweetener)
Sunflower oil
Tarragon (Estragon)
Tomato
Tomato dried
Tomato juice
Tomato paste
Tomato puree
Trout
Valerian
Vanilla
Vanilla pod
Vanilla powder
Vanilla sugar natural
Vegetable juice
Wakame
Watermelon
Wheat
Wheat bulgur
Wheat flakes
Wheat flatbread/pita bread
Wheat flour
Wheat flour whole grain
Wheat germ oil
Wheat semolina
Wheat semolina for children
White beans
Wormwood herb
Zucchini

10.2 Use ingredients: yes

Amaranth
Apple juice (natural cloudy)
Apple puree
Avocado
Bamboo shoots
Banana
Banana (cooking banana)
Barley
Barley flour
Barley grouts
Barley not peeled
Basic recipe for a duck soup

Basic recipe for a rice soup (Congee)
Batavia
Beans (green, fresh)
Black beans
Black tea
Blackberry leaves
Black-eyed peas
Breadcrumbs (wheat bread, bread roll)
Burdock root tea
Bush beans
Butter (half fat)
Butter beans white

Camembert
Cantaloupe
Capers in olive oil
Carambola (Star fruit)
Caviar
Chard
Chicken yolk
Chickweed
Coconut fat
Corn (roasted)
Corn germ oil
Corn starch
Crab
Cranberry
Créme fraiche cheese
Cress
Cucumber (spicy cucumber)
Dandelion juice
Dandelionroots tea
Elderberries
Fox nut, gorgon nut, makhana
Fresh cheese from soya
Freshwater fish
Gail plum
Ginkgo fruit
Ginseng root
Goose fat
Grapefruit (Pomelo)
Grapefruit juice
Grapeseed oil
Halibut (Flatfish)
Herbs various
Hijiki
Hokkaido pumpkin
Honey
Horehound leaves
Horse meat
Kidney beans (red)
Kiwi
Lamb's lettuce
Lemon
Lemon Balm (dried)
Lemon Balm (fresh)
Lemon juice
Lemon peel
Lettuce
Lima beans
Lime
Lime blossom tea
Loquate / Japanese medlar
Lotus seeds
Luo Han Guo fruit
Mango
Mango juice

Manioc flour
Maple syrup
Miso paste (soy bean paste)
Mulberry fruit
Mullet
Mung bean sprouting
Mussels
Noodles (wheat, lasagne) with egg
Noodles (wheat, ribbon noodles) with egg
Noodles (wheat, spaghetti) with egg
Noodles (whole grain) with egg
Olives
Olives green
Orange
Orange jam
Orange juice
Passion fruit
Peanut (roasted)
Peanut butter
Pearl barley
Pearl barley
Peas
Peppermint
Peppermint tea
Plum
Plum dried
Psyllium seed
Rabbit
Rabbit (wild)
Rabbit liver
Radish black
Raspberry leaf tea
Red beet
Rhubarb
Rice (fragrance)
Rice (Gaoliang / Sorghum)
Rice (whole grain)
Rice black
Rice flour
Rice mash
Rice noodles
Rice red
Rice round grain
Rice starch
Rice sticky
Rice sweet
Rice variety any
Rice wild (nature rice)
Rose blossom tea
Rusk
Salsify
Salt
Salt (herbal)

Savoy cabbage / kale
Seacrab
Sesame oil roasted
Sesame paste (Tahini)
Sesame, black
Sesame, white
Sorrel
Soy flour
Soy noodles
Soy sauce
Soy Tofu smoked
Soya Cuisine (soy cream)
Soybeans
Soybeans, blacks, fermented
Stevia (candyleaf, sweetleaf)
Sugar molasses
Sunflower seeds
Sweet potato
Thistle oil
Toast bread (whole grain)
Truffle
Tsampa (roasted barley flour)

Turmeric (yellow root)
Water
Water hot
Wheat beer
Wheat bran
Wheat/Rye/Gray-black bread with yeast
Wheatgrass powder
White bread (baguette)
White bread (pretzel sticks)
White bread (roll)
White bread (wheat bread)
White breadcrumbs
White cabbage
White dumpling bread (wheat bread cut into chunks)
Whole grain bread
Wholemeal flour
Wild garlic (garlic spinach)
Yarrow tea
Yeast
Yogurt (natural, 1.5% fat)
Yogurt (natural, 3.5% fat)

10.3 Use ingredients: little

Adzuki beans
Angelica root
Anise (Common Fennel)
Apple (sour)
Barley malt
Basic recipe for a beef soup
Basic recipe for a beef soup (warming)
Basic recipe for a fish soup
Bay leaf
Beef lungs (calf)
Berries of the season
Berry juice
Bitter Herb liqueur
Blackberry´s
Blueberry
Blueberry dried
Blueberry jam
Blueberry juice
Bulgur (cereals)
Buttermilk
Chives
Chocolate
Chocolate (Diabetic)
Clarified butter
Clementines
Clove
Codfish
Cooking oil
Coriander

Coriander (fresh)
Couscous
Cow's milk (1.5% fat)
Cow's milk (whole milk 3.5% fat)
Cranberry
Cranberry jam
Cranberry juice
Cream (30% fat)
Cream 10% coffee cream
Cream sour 10%
Cream sour 20%
Cream, sweet 30%
Cumin (Caraway seed)
Curcuma
Curd cheese 20%
Curd cheese 40%
Currant (black)
Currant (red)
Currant (white)
Currant jam (black)
Currant jam (red)
Currant juice (black)
Deer meat
Dill
Dulse (seaweed)
Eel
Fennel tea
Fresh cheese
Fresh cheese with herbs

Ginger fresh
Ginseng liqueur
Gooseberry
Grapes white
Ground
Ground caraway
Hawthorn
Kefir
King Solomon's-seal
Leek
Lentils
Lentils yellow
Lovage seeds
Lychee
Lychee in Preserved
Mackerel
Mallow (Malva sylvestris) blossom tea
Marjoram
Mayonnaise 50%
Mediterranean fish (cod, plaice, haddock, sea eel, mackerel)
Mineral water
Miso
Miso black (fermented)
Mozzarella
Multi-grain bread (gray bread)
Mustard
Mustard Dijon
Mustard medium hot
Mustard seeds
Mustard sweet
Nettles
Nori, purple seaweed, red algae
Onion (spring onion)
Onion read
Onion white
Parmesan
Parsley root
Pear juice
Pepper Cayenne
Pepper white (ground)
Peppercorns
Pheasant
Pigeon
Pineapple
Pineapple (from a can)
Pineapple juice without sugar
Pinto beans speckled
Plums
Pork fat (lard)
Pork ham
Pork ham cooked
Pork heart

Pork knuckle
Pork Lard
Pork liver
Pork meat
Pork skin
Pork stomach
Processed cheese 12%
Rabbit meat
Radish horseradish
Raspberry
Raspberry dried (immature)
Raspberry jam
Sauerkraut (cutted cabbage fermented)
Sour cherries
Sour cream 15% fat
Sour milk
Sour milk cheese 20%
Spelled (Dark) bread
Spelled flakes
Spelled grain
Spelled semolina
Spelled wholemeal flour
St. Benedict's thistle, blessed thistle, holy thistle, spotted thistle
Star anise
Strawberries
Strawberry Juice
Sugar - icing sugar
Sugar brown
Sugar candy white
Sugar cane sugar
Sugar fructose - fruit sugar
Sugar glucose - grapes sugar
Sugar Milk Sugar
Sugar white
Tangerine
Trout (smoked)
Turkey ham
Vinegar (Red wine vinegar)
Vinegar Aceto Balsamico white
Walnut oil
Wax gourd
Wild boar meat
Wormwood
Yam root, yam root tuber
Yoghurt vanilla

10.4 Do not use contra-acting foods

Almond
Almond marzipan
Almond milk
Almond puree
Anchovy / Sardine
Apricot
Apricot dried
Apricot jam
Apricot nectar
Apricots
Apricots juice
Basic recipe for a chicken soup
(warming)
Basil
Basil (fresh)
Bean oil
Beef bone marrow
Beef fillet
Beef heart
Beef heart (calf)
Beef kidney
Beef meat
Beef meatbones
Beef Oxtail pieces
Beef soup meat
Beef stomach
Blackberry dried (unripe fruit)
Blackberry jam
Boxhorn clover seeds
Cardamom
Carrot
Carrot (Early Carrot)
Carrot juice without sugar
Cereal coffee
Cherry
Cherry (sour)
Cherry compote
Cherry juice
Chestnuts
Chicken heart
Chicken liver
Chicken meat
Chili (pod or ground)
Cinnamon ground
Cinnamon sticks
Cocoa
Coconut milk
Cod
Coffee
Cream sour 30%
Curry

Curry paste red
Dates dried
Dates red
Deer meat
Dyer's broom herb
Eel smoked
Fennel
Fennel seeds ground
Feta cheese
French beans
Garlic
Ginger oil
Ginger powder
Goat
Goat and sheep's milk
Goat cheese
Goose egg
Grass carp
Green spelt
Hyssop
Juniper berry
Kumquats
Lamb bones
Lamb meat
Lamb shoulder
Lamb's lettuce
Lobster
Longane
Lovage
Lychee liqueur
Mayonnaise 80%
Mold cheese
Mutton
Mutton
Nutmeg
Oat
Oat flakes (whole grain)
Oat flakes roasted
Oat flour
Oat fusion (baby food)
Oat meal
Oat milk
Okra
Onion (shallot)
Oregano dried
Oregano fresh
Oyster mushroom
Papaya
Parsley
Peaches
Peaches (canned)

Pepper powder (hot)
Pepperoni
Pepperoni, red, pitted, halved
Pepperoni, yellow, pitted, halved
Peppers powder
Pickle
Pimento
Plaice
Pomegranate
Poppy
Pork Bacon
Pork ham smoked
Pork kidneys
processed cheese 30%
Pumpkin
Pumpkin seed oil
Radish
Radish (white, green, purple-red)
Raisins
Red wine
Rice malt
Rose hip
Rose hip tea
Rosemary

Sago (cereals)
Sake
Sheep's milk
Sheep's milk yoghurt
Shrimp
Shrimps
Soybean oil
Spiny lobsters
Spurdog (spiny dogfish, Schillerlocken)
Tabasco
Thyme
Thyme dried
Tuna
Turkey breast meat
Umeboshi paste
Umeboshi plums (Japanese apricots)
Vinegar (Apple vinegar)
Vinegar Aceto Balsamico
Walnuts
Walnuts roasted
White wine
Yarrow
Yogi tea

11 Complementary

11.1 Barberry roots

Berberis
Preparation: Healing tea (infusion)
Clears heat, dries moisture. Regulates liver-qi, clears lung-heat / mucus-heat, cools stomach fire.
Strengthens and strengthens the liver. Effective in liver disease, especially in jaundice and hepatitis. Immune System Stimulant, Digestive, removes protozoan parasites (amoebae), activates the thyroid gland and is considered to be one of the most beneficial herbs. One of the most effective herbs for correcting spleen, gall bladder and liver function, it is also effective against jaundice, gastritis, liver and kidney blockage and weakness. An effective stomach and intestinal and blood cleanser. It helps to remove blockages and deposits. Because it has antiseptic properties, it helps with liver problems.
Do not use in pregnancy.

11.2 Chicory roots

Cichorium intybus, rad.
Preparation: Decoction
Eliminates damp-heat. Eliminates heat from the liver, stomach and intestines. Regulates liver-qi, scatteres.
2-6 grams of finely chopped root are doused with 150 ml of cold water. Cook for 2 - 3 minutes and then strain. The tea is drunk ½ hour before the meal and should not be sweetened.
In rare cases, allergic skin reactions may occur.

11.3 Elderberry (flowers)

Sambucus nigra
Preparation: Decoction
Relieves wind-cold and wind-heat, soothes Shen.
Add 2 - 3 teaspoons of dried flowers to 150 ml of boiling water, cover for 3 - 5 min. Strain and drink as hot as possible. Drops that have collected in the lid into the tea, because here are also valuable ingredients.

11.4 Mint

Mentha arvensis
Preparation: Healing tea (infusion)
Eliminates internal heat, dispels wind-heat.
Pour 2-4 g with 250 ml of boiling water and let stand for 10 minutes. Then sieve. Drink in a single dose on an empty stomach.
Casting: Pour 1 g of powder with hot water, leave to simmer and then drink on an empty stomach, possibly sweeten the tea with a little honey;
Ointment: mix some mint powder with yellow vaseline, almond oil, lanolin or other fat base; then apply the cooling and soothing ointment to the head, chest, abdomen or other hot, painful, jammed or inflamed parts of the body.
Do not use on: severe shivering, nervous exhaustion.

12 Basics of Nutrition

The basic principles of nutrition described herein are general recommendations. They are not aimed at a specific form of therapy. Recommendations concerning a therapy have priority.

12.1 Nutrition

Regular meals in a relaxed atmosphere. A warm breakfast is considered a good start into the day.
The main meals ought to be taken for lunch – supper in the early evening. Pay attention to feeling hungry or sated: don't eat too much nor remain hungry is the rule
Prepare the meals freshly from natural, regional products. Frozen, heat-conserved, industrially prepared or foodstuffs cooked in the microwave oven are rejected.
Choice of foodstuffs according to the season: more cooling food in summer, more warming food in winter.
Eat cooked food at least twice a day. Food and drinks ought to be lukewarm, never ice-cold or hot.
Raw vegetables, briefly cooked vegetables, freshly squeezed juices and mineral water are not recommended. Milk and dairy products are only included in the diet if they don't cause problems. Don't use therapeutic recipes over a longer period without consulting your doctor or therapist.

Varied food
Enjoy the diversity of foodstuffs. Characteristics of a balanced nutrition are variety, suitable combination and a balanced quantity of rich and low energy foodstuffs (on one hand avoiding undersupply with essential nutrients and on the other hand to take to many undesirable substances).

A lot of Cereal Products - and Potatoes
Bread, pasta, rice, cereal flakes (best wholemeal) as well as potatoes contain almost no fat, but many vitamins, mineral nutrients, trace elements, roughage and secondary plant substances. These foodstuffs ought to be taken with low-fat side dishes.

Vegetables and Fruit – „Take Five" every day ... 5 portions of vegetables and fruit a day, as fresh as possible, briefly cooked, or maybe one portion as a juice – ideal as a side dish to every meal as well as snack between meals: Thus a lot of vitamins, mineral nutrients as well as roughage and secondary plant substances

Daily milk and dairy products
Milk and Dairy Products every Day, once or twice per Week Fish; meat, sausages as well as eggs moderately. These foodstuffs contain valuable nutrients like calcium in the milk, iodine selenium and omega-3 fat acids in saltwater fish. Meat is favorable due to its high content of disposable iron and the vitamins B1, B6 and B12. Quantities of 300 – 600 g meat and sausage per week are sufficient. Prefer low-fat products, especially in meat- and dairy products.

Low-fat and fatty Foodstuffs
Fat supplies us with essential fat acids and fatty foodstuffs contain also fat-soluble vitamins. Fat is high in energy; therefore much fat in the food may cause overweight, possibly also cancer. Too many saturated fat acids may further a tendency for cardio-vascular diseases in the long term. Prefer vegetable oils and fats (e.g. rapeseed-, olive-, soya-oils and solid fats produced therefrom). Beware of invisible fat in meat- and dairy products, pastry and sweets as well as in fast-food and convenience foods. 70 – 90 g fat per day is sufficient.

Moderately Sugar and Salt
Take sugar and foods/drinks containing various kinds of sugar (e.g. glucose syrup) only occasionally. Use herbs and spices as well as a little salt creatively. Prefer salt containing iodine.

Plenty of Liquids
Water is absolutely essential. Drink 1-2 l liquids every day. Prefer water (with or without gas) and other low-calorie drinks. Alcoholic drinks should not be taken.

Tasty Dishes, carefully cooked
Cook the meals with as low temperatures and as short as possible, using little water and fat – this preserves the original taste, keeps the nutrients intact and prevents the production of harmful compounds.

Take time and enjoy the food
Take your Time and enjoy your Food
Eating consciously helps to eat right. The eye enjoys food, too. It's fun, invites to enjoy varied dishes and stimulates the feeling of satiety.

Watch your Weight and stay in Motion
A balanced diet and a lot of exercise and sport (30 – 60 min/day) are a healthy combination. The right weight furthers well-being and health.

Thermals, directional effectiveness, digestive power
There are various criteria for judging the effectiveness of herbs and foodstuffs.
The use of certain herbs and ingredients is based on observations of the effects on the body which these foodstuffs, herbs and spices show after having eaten them. The medical science has developed following system: Every ingredient or herb has a directional effectiveness. Furthermore, there are herbs which have a special effect on certain organs.
The basic condition for a healthy metabolism is to obtain sufficient energy from food and that the digestive process doesn't use too much energy. An easily digestible meal makes content and sated, doesn't cause flatulence and fatigue after the meal. The perfect spices increase the healthiness of our meals. Very often, just small doses of herbs and spices will suffice. They are not used to make us sated, but to help our digestive organs to digest the food.

12.2 Recipes

The recipes list the ingredients to be used and the cooking instructions show how the dish is prepared. The list of ingredients shows the concerned quantities as well as the relevance for the therapy. If you find „omit", try to comply or find an alternative from the „list of recommended foodstuffs". Mostly it shall result just in a small change of taste when you simply avoid this ingredient.
Mild cooking methods: boiling, stewing, poaching, steaming
Strong cooking methods: barbecuing, roasting, frying, smoking
Balanced cooking methods: deep-frying, baking brick
Deep-freezing and warming in the microwave oven should be avoided (denaturalization).

12.3 Foodstuffs

Foodstuffs have an effect on body and soul like medicinal herbs, only a very much milder one. Dietary advice is mainly based on regional foodstuffs. The knowledge about the effects of each foodstuff and the knowledge, when which foodstuff shall be used, is based on the school medicine. Use ecologic-organic products, if possible. As everything should be cooked for a long time due to a better digestability and very rarely eaten raw, the food agrees with everyone.
The classification of the foodstuffs according to their effect on the body is the basis in order to achieve a harmonious status of health.
Dietary advisors do not recommend certain foodstuffs for everyone. The individual diet is tailor-made for the individual constitution.

Buy only fresh and ripe fruit and vegetables. You ought to leave unripe fruit and vegetables and such with brown spots and wilted leaves behind in the market. In this case take deep-frozen goods (never ready-to-serve dishes!). Fruit and vegetables are deep-frozen immediately after harvesting and often contain more vitamins and minerals than the goods from the vegetable shelf. Whereas conserved or tinned goods contain very much less biological substances. Also, salt, sugar and others are mostly added to the latter. Never leave the foodstuffs in the water after washing them to avoid that many vital substances get drowned. Clean salads, fruit and vegetables immediately before serving.

Please make sure of the hygienic processing of foodstuffs. Clean your salads, fruit and vegetables carefully. When cooking with meat, prepare all ingredients first and then process the meat products. Clean the worktop and tools very carefully. Wooden surfaces ought to be treated with a mild disinfectant regularly in order to reduce germination. Store fruit and vegetables separately, if possible. Harvested fruit and vegetables are still alive and emit e.g. ethylene gas, which makes other products ripen and age faster. Keep meat and fish in the closed packaging or store them in the fridge in closed containers.

12.4 Herbs

There are some basic rules for storing medicinal herbs. On principle, herbs must be protected from direct sunlight, humidity and heat.

Containers for the storage of herbs may be glasses, ceramic jars and even plastic containers. However, plastic is a rather unsuitable material and should only be a short-term solution. In case of glass containers, use a dark material.

Medicinal herbs cannot be kept for any long period. The shelf life of herbs is limited. However, it can be prolonged with suitable storage. The place should be dark, rather cool and absolutely dry. A wooden medicine cabinet, placed not directly next to a source of heat, would be ideal. Never buy large quantities of herbs so as not to have to throw them away. Label the container with the name of the herb and the date of harvesting or processing.

13 Other dietic-books

The following syndromes of dietetics, TCM or for a therapy supplement for cancer are available.

Dietetics

E001. Nutrition of the infant - baby food
E002. Nutrition during lactation
E003. Nutrition in old age
E004. Nutrition of children and adolescents
E005. Nutrition of athletes
E006. Light weight
E007. Pregnancy
E008. Full food

Protein and electrolyte - kidneys
E009. (hemodialysis) dialysis treatment
E010. Acute renal failure
E011. Chronic renal insufficiency
E012. Nephrotic syndrome
E013. Kidney stones (nephrolithiasis)

Gastrointestinal tract - pancreas
E014. Acute pancreatitis (inflammation of the pancreas)
E015. Chronic pancreatitis (inflammation of the pancreas)

Gastrointestinal tract - small intestine and large intestine
E016. Acute obstipation (constipation)
E017. Chronic obstipation (constipation)
E018. Colon irritabile
E019. Diverticulitis
E020. Acquired lactose intolerance (lactose malabsorption)
E021. Fructose malabsorption
E022. Glutensensitive enteropathy (celiac disease)
E023. Colectomy
E024. Short Bowel Syndrome

Gastrointestinal tract - liver, gallbladder, bile ducts
E025. Acute and chronic hepatitis (inflammation of the liver)
E026. Cholelithiasis (bile stones)
E027. fatty liver
E028. cirrhosis

Gastrointestinal tract - Stomach and duodenal intestine
E029. Acute gastritis
E030. Chronic gastritis
E031. Stomach bleeding
E032. Ulcus ventriculi and duodenal ulcer
E033. Condition after gastric surgery

Gastrointestinal tract - oral cavity and esophagus
E034. Stomatitis
E035. Esophageal carcinoma (esophageal cancer)
E036. Refluosophagitis (heartburn)

Special diseases
E037. Phenylketonuria (PKU)
E038. Rheumatic joint diseases

Metabolism
E039. Obesity (overweight)
E040. Diabetes mellitus
E041. Eating disorders (underweight)

Fat metabolism
E042. Hypercholesterolaemia (increased cholesterol level)
E043. Hepatic Encephalopathy

Heart and circulation
E044. Arteriosclerosis (arterial calcification)
E045. Heart insufficiency
E046. Hypertension
E047. Hyperuricaemia and gout

Changed nutrient requirements
E048. In case of fever
E049. For malignant diseases
E050. After burns
E051. Radiation and chemotherapy

CANCER
E100. Pancreatic cancer
E101. Bladder cancer
E102. Blood cancer (leukemia)
E103. Breast cancer
E104. Colorectal cancer
E105. Gastric cancer
E106. Kidney cancer
E107. Esophageal cancer

TCM
E200. Bladder - moisture heat in the bladder
E201. Bladder - moisture and cold in the bladder
E202. Bladder - emptiness and cold in the bladder
E203. Large intestine - external cold affects the large intestine
E204. Large intestine - moisture heat in the large intestine
E205. Large intestine - heat blocks the intestine II acute
E206. Large intestine - dryness of the colon
E207. Large intestine - Yang deficiency (cold)
E208. Heart - Blood insufficiency
E209. Heart - Blood stagnation
E210. Heart - Fire
E211. Heart - Hot mucus clogs the heart pores

E212. Heart - Cold mucus clogs the heart pores
E213. Heart - Qi deficiency
E214. Heart - Yang deficiency
E215. Heart - Yin deficiency
E216. Liver - Ascending Liver Yang
E217. Liver - Blood deficiency
E218. Liver - Blood stagnation
E219. Liver - Moisture heat in liver and gall bladder
E220. Liver - Fire
E221. Liver - Gall bladder Qi-Empty
E222. Liver - Cold in the liver meridian
E223. Liver - Qi stagnation
E224. Liver - Wind
E225. Liver - Wind with ascending liver Yang
E226. Liver - Wind with blood anemic
E227. Liver - Wind with extreme heat
E228. Lung - Qi deficiency
E229. Lung - Mucus-moisture in the lungs
E230. Lung - Mucus-heat in the lungs
E231. Lung - Mucus-cold in the lungs
E232. Lung - Dryness of the lungs
E233. Lung - Wind-heat attacks the lungs
E234. Lung - Wind-cold affects the lungs
E235. Lung - Yin deficiency
E236. Stomach - Bloodstagnation
E237. Stomach - Fire
E238. Stomach - Cold with liquid
E239. Stomach - Nutrition stagnation
E240. Stomach - Qi deficiency
E241. Stomach - Rebellious Qi
E242. Stomach - Yin Emptiness
E243. Spleen - Heat and moisture attack the spleen
E244. Spleen - Coldness and moisture affects the spleen
E245. Spleen - Qi deficiency
E246. Spleen - Qi deficiency + Declining spleen Qi
E247. Spleen - Qi deficiency + spleen does not control the blood
E248. Spleen - Yang deficiency
E249. Kidney - Heart and kidney no longer communicate
E250. Kidney - Jing deficiency
E251. Kidney - Kidneys cannot receive the Qi
E252. Kidney - Qi is not stable
E253. Kidney - Yang deficiency
E254. Kidney - Yin deficiency

For further information visit nutribook.info.

14 EBNS - Software for nutritional counseling

The main task of the database is to create personalized nutritional advice for each patient individually. The database was developed for Dietetics and Traditional Chinese Medicine.

The Database supports training and advices in the daily work routine.

The computer program provides lists of recipes, ingredients and herbs, which are given to the client. individually adjustable according to patient's request from whole food to vegetarians (lacto, ovo, ...). For every register there is an information sheet which can be given to the client. All texts can be individually designed.

The syndromes can be combined and result in an intersection of the recommended recipes and ingredients. The automated diagnosis for the TCM enables you to check your experience during the training as well as to confirm your diagnosis in the working day. You select several predefined symptoms and have the program automatically display the relevant syndromes.

How to work with the database:
Select the patient / client, select one or more of the syndromes you diagnosed and print the folder.

You can change all values, create new symptoms or syndromes, develop recipes, change or adapt ingredients and herbs to your findings. In simple client management, all relevant data about the person is stored. You get an overview of the past diagnoses and the development of the course of the disease.

As a consultant you save a lot of time when you print out the recipe, food and herbal lists for the recognized syndromes and give them to the clients. You can use this time for a personal conversation. With the database, dieticians and nutritionists can view the nutrients and trace elements for each recipe and develop recipes for syndromes even with suggested ingredients.

All recipe and grocery lists can also be ordered from me as a combination of several diseases. I wish all readers good luck, health and happiness in life.
More information can be found at www.ebns.at.
Volunteer: www.krebsinfo.at
Josef Miligui